Negotiating for Business Results

JUDITH E. FISHER, PH. D.

Business Skills Express Series

IRWIN
Professional Publishing

MIRROR PRESS

Burr Ridge, Illinois
New York, New York
Boston, Massachusetts

This symbol indicates that the paper in this book is made of recycled paper. Its fiber content exceeds the recommended minimum of 50% waste paper fibers as specified by the EPA.

© RICHARD D. IRWIN, INC., 1994

Mirror Press:	David R. Helmstadter
	Carla F. Tishler
Editor-in-Chief:	Jeffrey A. Krames
Marketing manager:	Lynn M. Kalanik
Project editor:	Stephanie M. Britt
Production manager:	Diane Palmer
Designer:	Jeanne Rivera
Art manager:	Kim Meriwether
Compositor:	Alexander Graphics
Typeface:	12/14 Criterion
Printer:	Malloy Lithographing, Inc.

Library of Congress Cataloging-in-Publication Data

Fisher, Judith E.
    Negotiating for business results / Judith E. Fisher.
      p.   cm.—(Business skills express series)
    ISBN 0-7863-0114-7
    1. Negotiation in business. I. Title. II. Series.
    HD58.6.F57 1994
    658.4—dc20

                                       93–41065

Printed in the United States of America
  2 3 4 5 6 7 8 9 0 ML 0 9 8 7 6 5 4

PREFACE

Negotiation is usually associated with the world of business, but its impact is really much wider. It affects family relationships, personal lives, and community interactions. Negotiating is more than a business skill; it's an essential skill for coping with the challenges of daily life.

This book focuses on negotiation skills. Whether your work is centered on negotiation—selling, handling complaints, arbitrating disputes—or whether you simply negotiate to make things happen on the job, this book has something for you.

- If you're new to the business world, this book can help you learn the fundamentals of business negotiation and open your eyes to the potential for using negotiation in your daily life.
- If you're an experienced businessperson, this book can help you refine your negotiating skills, enabling you to make your work life and home life more manageable through negotiation.

This book is organized into seven chapters. Each chapter presents an important topic or skill set related to negotiation. Chapter 1 answers the fundamental question, What is negotiation? Chapter 2 presents the critical elements in negotiation and provides insight into the traits of a successful negotiator. Chapter 3 describes a general process model for negotiation; in subsequent chapters, key steps are explained in more detail.

Chapter 4 focuses on preparing for negotiations. Chapter 5 looks at the role of communications skills in the negotiation process. Chapter 6 reviews selected negotiation techniques—tried-and-true approaches that you're likely to encounter in negotiations sessions. Finally, Chapter 7 gives you a wide selection of tips and tactics for negotiating effectively in a variety of situations. The book ends with a review test and recommendations for sharpening your skills.

This book can be used in a variety of ways, as part of a training session at work, in an adult-education class, or during an offsite seminar or workshop. In those cases, your group leader will give you specific directions on how to use this book. Or you may be using this book as part of your own personal job skills improvement plan. In that case, you are in control of the learning experience. You decide which chapters you want to tackle. You decide when, where, and how long to study. To make the most of this self-study learning experience:

- Schedule some uninterrupted time. Set aside half an hour, or tell yourself you'll finish a chapter.

- Eliminate distractions.

- Work through the book with a pencil. Read the text and do the exercises. Write your answers and record your thoughts in the book. Take notes in the margins or highlight important ideas.

- Ask yourself:
  How does this idea fit in with my job?
  How could I apply this technique or use this idea?
  How could I adapt these tips or tactics to fit my situation?

Remember, what you get out of this book is directly related to the effort put into using it.

Judith E. Fisher

ABOUT THE AUTHOR

Judith E. Fisher, PhD, is President of Education and Training Consultants, Inc., in Riverview, Florida. As a consultant, Dr. Fisher specializes in design, development, and production of education and training materials for the adult learner in business and industry. Her client roster includes Hilton Hotels, Inter-Continental Hotels, Marriott Hotels, MCI, Northern Telecom, Xerox, and IBM. Dr. Fisher is the recipient of several awards, including the National Endowment for the Humanities Fellowship and an appointment to Outstanding Educators of America. She completed her doctoral work in Instructional Design and Development.

ABOUT IRWIN PROFESSIONAL PUBLISHING

Irwin Professional Publishing is the nation's premier publisher of business books. As a Times Mirror company, we work closely with Times Mirror training organizations, including Zenger-Miller, Inc.; Learning International, Inc., and Kaset International to serve the training needs of business and industry.

About the Business Skills Express Series

This expanding series of authoritative, concise, and fast-paced books delivers high-quality training on key business topics at a remarkably affordable cost. The series will help managers, supervisors, and frontline personnel in organizations of all sizes and types hone their business skills while enhancing job performance and career satisfaction.

Business Skills Express books are ideal for employee seminars, independent self-study, on-the-job training, and classroom-based instruction. Express books are also convenient-to-use references at work.

CONTENTS

Self-Assessment

How confident are you about your negotiating skills? Here's an opportunity to analyze your negotiating strengths and weaknesses. For each statement, mark the appropriate space. Be honest with yourself.

	Almost Always	Sometimes	Almost Never
1. I remain calm under pressure.	_____	_____	_____
2. I can think rationally even when someone tries to rile my emotions.	_____	_____	_____
3. I think everything is negotiable.	_____	_____	_____
4. I believe both parties should win in a negotiation.	_____	_____	_____
5. I routinely use effective questioning to uncover information in negotiations.	_____	_____	_____
6. In negotiations, I listen as much or more than I speak.	_____	_____	_____
7. I observe and interpret body language in negotiation sessions.	_____	_____	_____
8. I carefully prepare for each negotiation.	_____	_____	_____
9. I am adept at recognizing and combating negotiating tactics.	_____	_____	_____
10. I can use timing techniques to advantage in a negotiation.	_____	_____	_____
11. I always seek common ground and then consider alternatives in negotiations.	_____	_____	_____
12. I think of negotiation as an opportunity to reach agreement.	_____	_____	_____

There are no right or wrong answers. Your goal should be to change your *almost never* responses to either *sometimes* or *almost always* by the time you've finished this book.

1

What Is Negotiation?

This chapter will help you to:

- Consider varying views of negotiation.
- Distinguish between confrontation and cooperation in negotiation.
- Develop a working definition for negotiation.

Linda is looking forward to her 10th class reunion in June. All her plans are in place—travel arrangements, party clothes, social engagements . . . the works. Unfortunately, her manager has just identified a conflict in vacation schedules. Linda and a co-worker, Tom, have requested the same two-week vacation period. The company says one of them must change vacation dates. The manager, hoping to avoid the difficult decision on who has to change dates, says that Linda and Tom should work this out themselves. What can they do? ■

DEFINING NEGOTIATION

It's curious. Most people believe they know what negotiation is, but when you ask them to define it, responses vary widely.

Start with Your Own Ideas

How would you define negotiation?

_____

_____

_____

_____

_____

1

Consider Other Possibilities

Suppose you asked 10 people to define negotiation. These ideas represent the various responses you might receive. As you look over the definitions, compare and contrast them. What do they have in common? How do they differ?

Negotiation Is . . .

- Conferring with another in bargaining or trade.
- Overcoming obstacles to make a deal.
- Discussing options to reach an agreement.
- Making progress toward a desired goal or objective.
- Arriving at a mutually agreeable solution to a problem.
- Finding out what the other person wants and then making him or her believe you are providing it.
- Waging a contest of wills or a battle of wits.
- Attempting to get what you want.
- Persuading someone to do as you wish or to go along with your ideas.
- Wheeling and dealing.

What common ideas run through these definitions?

_____

_____

_____

Every definition states or implies some kind of action. Most of the definitions clearly indicate that more than one person is involved. The majority of definitions have an underlying sense of communication.

What major differences do you notice among these definitions?

_____

_____

_____

Some definitions seem to focus on cooperation, but others imply some level of confrontation. Some definitions point out a purpose or goal, others do not.

In a minute, we'll pull these diverse ideas into a working definition for negotiation. But first, let's look at a very important concept in negotiation—confrontation versus cooperation. We are going to consider what negotiation is and what it isn't.

What Negotiation Isn't

Some people believe that a negotiation is like a contest or game—a tug o' war, for example. They believe that in a negotiation there is only one winner, and that means there also must be a loser.

Where did they get this idea? Some people are simply confrontational or aggressive by nature and view negotiations as a chance to test their mettle. Others feel that negotiations are opportunities to demonstrate their superiority. Still others probably got the idea of winning and losing negotiations from personal experience. Unfortunately, many of us have had negotiating experiences in which we felt as though we'd been tricked or outsmarted.

Nevertheless, negotiation does not require confrontation. It is not an intellectual sparring match where one side raises its glove in victory when the other side falls to the floor. Negotiation need not be adversarial at all.

1

What Negotiation Is

There is another viewpoint. Many people think of negotiation as a way of forging an agreement. They seem naturally inclined to compromise. They do not think in terms of winner and loser. Instead, they think in terms of mutual satisfaction—with both sides winning.

Negotiation should really be an act of cooperation and not a confrontation. Think of negotiation as an opportunity to work together to achieve a mutual goal that would have been impossible for one person working alone.

A Practical Definition of Negotiation

Let's return to the common elements from those sample definitions. Some key words are: *action, process, communication, agreeable, solutions,* and *options.* These become a working definition:

Negotiation is a communication process between two or more people in which they consider alternatives to arrive at mutually agreeable solutions or reach mutually satisfactory objectives.

THE CONTEXT OF NEGOTIATION

With a workable definition for negotiation, we can think about the context for negotiations. Consider these key questions.

- Who negotiates?
- Where do negotiations occur?
- What's negotiable?
- Why negotiate?

Who Negotiates?

Our working definition of negotiation is broad. If you were thinking that only lawyers and labor leaders negotiate, broaden your horizons. In the list below, check off those who negotiate.

_____	Elected officials.
_____	Lawyers.
_____	College students.
_____	Corporate officers.
_____	Directors on a board.
_____	Members of a committee.
_____	A jury.
_____	Married couples.
_____	Laborers.
_____	Business managers.
_____	Customer service representatives.
_____	Salespeople.
_____	Customers.
_____	Toddlers, children, and teenagers.
_____	Friends.
_____	Families.

———— Countries.

———— Labor leaders.

———— Parents.

———— Buyers or agents.

Within the context of our working definition, everyone in the list negotiates at some time. You can safely say that *everyone negotiates*.

Where Do Negotiations Occur?

Negotiations may occur in any business—an auto body shop, a law firm, an insurance agency, a real estate sales office, a retail clothing store. Similarly, negotiations typically take place in a range of business settings—your office, your manager's office, a customer's premises, or the reception area. However, negotiations are also likely to occur among family members in the home or among friends in other social settings. Negotiations can and do take place almost *anywhere*.

What's Negotiable?

What situations tend to precipitate negotiations? The key here is conflict. Any situation where there is real or perceived conflict between two or more people is ripe for negotiation.

Consider planning a weekend outing. You want to go to the baseball game, but your companion wants to attend an outdoor art festival. This may be a minor conflict, but it is a conflict. It's an occasion ripe for negotiation.

Think about the last time you needed a raise. You wanted to figure out a way to get more spendable income each month, but your manager or employer did not seem willing to give you a raise in salary. Again, a perceived conflict is an occasion for negotiation.

Finally, consider a more global example. The United States wanted to develop an agreement with the then USSR to control and reduce nuclear armaments. There were major conflicts in philosophy, military outlook, and perceived power. Each side had interests it wanted to protect. The obvious solution—negotiate.

1

Those three examples should have triggered some ideas about what kinds of conflicts might be negotiable. Check the items in the list that are negotiable.

_____ Price of a pair of shoes in a retail store.

_____ An insurance settlement.

_____ Sharing resources.

_____ Schedule for completing a construction project.

_____ Your child's weekly allowance.

_____ The allocation of household chores.

_____ Real estate salesperson's commission.

_____ Peace treaties.

_____ Terms of a lease agreement.

_____ A contract to provide consulting services.

_____ The sale of used furniture.

_____ Disposal of assets in bankruptcy.

_____ Allocation of property in divorce.

_____ Conditions at the workplace.

_____ The vacation schedule at work.

_____ Bills that will be voted on by Congress.

_____ The purchase of an automobile.

_____ The timelines on a major project.

As you can see, any situation where there is conflict can be appropriate for negotiation. Whenever people meet to draw up contracts, make buying or selling transactions, settle differences, or develop working relationships, the name of the game is negotiation. _Everything is negotiable_!

Why Negotiate?

Negotiation is, first of all, a civilized method of conflict resolution. But it is also more than that. It is a skill that will enable you to enrich both your working life and your personal life by helping you meet your goals and objectives and satisfy your needs.

Remembering When

Sometimes negotiation results can be exceptionally positive.

- Do you recall the wonderful deal you made for that investment property?
- How about the extra days off you negotiated last year?
- Remember the magnificent compromise you worked out with your teenager about using the family car?

Other times, results may be less than outstanding.

- Remember that embarrassingly inept deal you made at the auto dealership?
- What about the time your teenager wheedled you into agreeing to chaperone the after-prom party?
- How about when you couldn't say no to a co-worker's request for extra help even when your workload was already heavy?

Looking Ahead

If you could remember all of the negotiations you've made in your lifetime, would you say you've had more successes than failures? Or is your negotiation experience skewed in the other direction?

Frankly, most people would like to improve their negotiation batting average, increase their success rate, and minimize their failures, but are not exactly sure how to go about it.

Chapter 1 Checkpoints

Review the key points in the quiz. When you have finished the quiz, check your answers.

1. Write a definition for negotiation. Use your own words.

_____

_____

_____

_____

_____

_____

_____

2. Someone once said: "Conflict is at the heart of negotiation." Explain that idea in your own words.

_____

_____

_____

_____

_____

_____

_____

3. Who negotiates?

_____

4. Where do negotiations occur?

_____

5. What's negotiable?

_____

6. Why negotiate?

_____

_____

_____

Checkpoint 1 Feedback

Check your answers by referring to the ideas below.

1. Here is one definition of negotiation:

Negotiation is a communication process between two or more people in which they consider alternatives to arrive at mutually agreeable solutions or reach mutually satisfactory objectives.

Your definition may be different, but it should have the same basic elements and meaning.

2. Here is one explanation:

Any situation of conflict between two or more people is a possible opportunity for negotiation. Negotiation may begin in conflict, but it should end in cooperation.

Your wording may be different, but the idea should be the same.

3. Everyone.
4. Everywhere.
5. Everything.
6. To resolve conflict; to advance your own goals/objectives.

2

The Elements of Negotiation

This chapter will help you to:

- Identify the primary goal of negotiation.
- Describe the three critical elements in negotiation.
- Explain the perception of strength or power in negotiation.

Linda was steamed when she found out about the conflict in vacation schedules. As she left work that day, she saw Tom Evans in the parking lot, and he wasn't smiling either. Normally cordial, Tom didn't even wave. "Oh boy," thought Linda, "how are we ever going to settle this problem! Neither one of us wants to lose, but only one can take a vacation the first two weeks in June." ■

THE GOAL OF NEGOTIATING: DEVELOPING AGREEMENT

No matter what kind of conflict you plan to resolve through negotiation, there is one major goal. The objective in negotiation is to forge an agreement where there was once a conflict. Therefore, negotiation may begin with tension, anxiety, or disagreement over interests and issues, but successful negotiations will end with a mutually agreeable solution or compromise.

It's Not Just Win or Lose

Avoid thinking of negotiation as a game or a contest. This approach promotes the idea that one side will win and the other will lose. Neither winning at all costs nor merely defeating the opponent is a legitimate goal for negotiations. This line of thinking can lead you into perilous waters.

An example is the well-known situation where workers virtually force management to provide a large pay raise. The workers may have won the negotiation, and the company owners lost. But when the company doesn't earn enough to fund the pay raises, what happens? Workers are laid off. Was the negotiated win at all costs really worth it?

Another example involves the compulsion to defeat the opponent, pure and simple. Two manufacturers were negotiating competitively for a limited supply of resource material available for immediate shipment. The rivalry between the two manufacturers had grown over years of sales competition until it almost took on a life of its own. Thus, one manufacturer bid an outrageously high price for the material, knowing his competitor could not meet it. He defeated the opponent, won the negotiation, and obtained the resource, but the costs prevented him from making a profit and ruined the financial performance of the company for that quarter. In negotiations, such egotism can be a very expensive habit.

Cooperation Makes a Difference

What might have happened in these two situations if the parties had recognized the real objective of negotiations? What if the focus was shifted from competing head-on to cooperating side-by-side?

In the first case, the workers and management might have been able to cooperate in developing a mutually satisfactory plan. For instance, they might have formulated a pay increase tied to improved productivity or profitability of the company. That might satisfy the workers' need for more money and management's need for additional production or increased profits.

In the second case, the difference would be immediately apparent to any impartial observer. The rivalry interfered with rational problem solving and effectively prevented any real negotiations from taking place. By cooperating, the manufacturers may have agreed to split the resources in some equitable way, which would have enabled both to continue production.

Remember that negotiation is cooperation—you and the other side working together. Cooperation usually leads to conflict resolution.

Win–Win Negotiation

As the previous examples show, both sides in a negotiation can be winners, providing they work toward the real objective—arriving at a solution that is mutually agreeable or acceptble. The negotiating sides should be satisfied with the negotiated outcome. This does not necessarily mean that each side achieved 100 percent of its desired outcomes in negotiation. But it does mean that both sides see the value in the negotiated solution and are willing to accept it.

This type of negotiation is often called win–win negotiation because both sides win when the conflict is resolved through compromise. There simply are no losers.

Think of negotiation as the resolution of differences to the mutual benefit of all parties. It might be considered both an art and a science. It is the science of cooperative compromise, and it is the art of collaborative agreement.

Hint

Edmund Burke, the 18th-century British statesman and orator, has observed:

> All government—indeed, every human benefit and enjoyment, every virtue, and every prudent act—is founded on compromise and barter.

As you can see, win–win negotiation is not a new concept. Compromise has always been a fundamental feature of civilized societies, and win–win negotiations build on that base.

CRITICAL ELEMENTS IN NEGOTIATION

In order to negotiate successfully, you'll need to become aware of several critical elements and how they affect your negotiating effort.

- Knowledge or information.
- Time or deadline pressure.
- Strength or power.

For the sake of discussion, we will talk about each of these elements separately. But in an actual negotiation session, they are usually intertwined.

Knowledge or Information

The more you know about a situation—the more information you have—the more likely you are to succeed in a negotiation. Knowledge is an essential ally.

Why is information so important in negotiation? Because it enables you to think of alternatives, invent options, develop effective strategies, and deploy tactics, the more knowledge you have, the better your basis for negotiation.

What kind of knowledge do you need? You might begin by knowing yourself. You must be fully aware of your own desires, needs, and objectives in the negotiation. Take stock of your own strengths and weaknesses in the negotiating environment. Review your negotiating parameters, like time limits, margins for acceptable give and take, or the predetermined increments of deal making. Decide on a bottom line—the point at which it is no longer worth the effort to continue negotiating, when it's preferable to walk away without reaching agreement.

Then you may turn your attention to finding out about the other side. Ideally, you'll find out everything you can about the person doing the negotiating, and that includes both personal and business information. Then you'll analyze the other side much as you analyzed your own side. What are the desires, needs, and objectives of the other side? What are their negotiating strengths and weaknesses, parameters, and bottom line?

You'll use that information to gain an advantage in negotiation. With broad and detailed knowledge, you are in an excellent position to identify areas where you are already in agreement and to locate areas where you need to negotiate an agreement. Your knowledge will enable you to think creatively about the negotiation process and all of its variables.

Let's consider an example that illustrates how knowledge can make a direct impact on negotiations. Suppose you have negotiated an astonishingly good price for a new automobile—$2,000 less than you thought you'd have to pay. After making the deal, you begin to wonder why it seemed so easy. A few days later, you read an article on the automaker's plans to introduce a totally redesigned model within a few months.

How did knowledge or lack of knowledge affect this negotiation?

_____

_____

_____

You didn't do your homework before you entered the final negotiation for the car, so you were unaware of the soon-to-be-released new product. Worse yet, you didn't ask the salesperson any direct questions about new models, so the salesperson's knowledge about the debut of a brand new design simply never surfaced. Your lack of knowledge about a key factor in the deal diminished the strength of your negotiation.

Time or Deadline Pressure

The second critical factor in negotiation is time or deadline pressure. For most people, the time factor in negotiation—a deadline for performance—adds a tremendous amount of pressure to an already tense situation.

To understand how time enters into the negotiation process, let's analyze typical deadline behavior. When your manager gives you a deadline, what is your reaction? If you're typical, you'll ignore the time factor until the deadline nears. Then you'll panic and rush the job through to meet the deadline at the last moment. In effect, the deadline may have put pressure on you originally, but your own delaying tactics have increased the pressure to the point of desperation.

If you knew the other side's deadline pressures, what advantage might that offer you in the negotiation process? When you can control your own deadline pressures while exploiting those of the other side, you will be able to control the progress of the negotiations.

Consider an example. Your office lease is expiring at the end of the quarter when the building is scheduled for demolition. You are shopping for new premises, have identified an office park where you'd like to relocate, and must negotiate a lease within 30 days. The leasing agent is unaware of your time pressure. Who's in the driver's seat for this negotiation?

How does deadline pressure affect the negotiating process in this example?

_____

_____

_____

You're in the driver's seat on this one, as long as the agent does not become aware of your time pressure. You must manage your own deadline. Once the agent discovers your deadline, however, your negotiating strength wanes because the agent knows the clock is running and time is on his or her side. The agent knows you'll have to forge an agreement—at virtually the last minute—in order to beat the relocation deadline. That's how deadlines can affect a negotiated agreement.

Strength or Power

The third critical factor in negotiation is strength, or power. In the context of negotiation, strength might be defined as the ability to influence or control the participants and the events.

In negotiation, strength is often rooted in knowledge. Strength is gained from the difference between what you know about the other side's situation versus what the other side knows about your situation.

The balance of power in a negotiation is not static. It may shift frequently from one side to the other as information is revealed and time deadlines approach. Of course, you'd like to maintain the balance of power in favor of your side, while the other side hopes to sway the balance of power into its camp. As long as these power shifts occur, see-sawing back and forth, the negotiation process is likely to continue.

When does the negotiation process wind down? There are two strength/power situations that will tend to close negotiations: a radically out-of-balance condition, and a totally balanced condition. Let's explore each briefly.

When one side perceives the other as having gained the vast majority (or all) of the power, the negotiation will soon end, but the result will probably not be a happy one. The side that has lost all power often feels abused, cheated, or tricked. An agreement arising out of these conditions is not a win–win solution.

In contrast, agreement reached when there is a *perceived* balance of power is more likely to promote the win–win feeling. When both sides perceive a balance of power, compromise becomes the next logical step, and the negotiation will soon be concluded and mutually satisfactory.

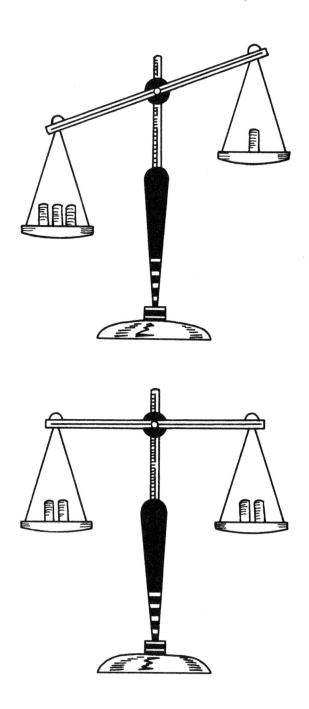

Hint

Based on the three critical negotiation elements, three rules of thumb usually apply:

- The party with the most accurate and relevant *knowledge* (information) is likely to prevail.
- The party with the earliest *deadline* (most time pressure) generally has the weaker position.
- The parties must strive to balance their *strengths* (power) to encourage compromise and drive toward a win-win resolution.

Think about It

Think about the balance of power in negotiation. Relate each of the situations below to your own negotiation experiences. Jot down relevant examples from either business or personal negotiations.

1. *Power may be real or assumed.* If one side assumes the other has an advantage, it makes no difference whether the advantage is real or not. *My example*:

_____

_____

_____

2. *Power is effective only if the negotiators are aware of it.* Suppose your customer needs your product because it is the only one that will work for her. That knowledge would give you power, an advantage in the negotiation process. But, unfortunately, you don't know that fact, so you don't really have the power. *My example*:

_____

_____

_____

2

3. *Power is effective only if it is acknowledged.* The president of a large corporation may think his position gives him an advantage in negotiating with you. However, if you are not intimidated, there is no advantage, and his power is nullified. *My example*:

---

4. *Power need not actually be used to be effective.* You might be afraid that a long-time customer won't continue to buy from you unless you give price concessions. Even though the customer hasn't threatened to use this advantage, it's still working for him. *My example*:

---

5. *Using power may be risky.* You may have acquired the balance of power in a negotiation, but wielding that power may have negative consequences. For instance, you might drive a hard bargain and get your co-workers to work through their lunch breaks this week to get a project out the door, but wielding that power may ruin a long-term working relationship. *My example*:

Chapter 2 Checkpoints

Mark each statement T for true or F for false. When you finish check your answers.

_____ 1. Negotiation is a process designed to resolve conflicts.

_____ 2. The goal of all negotiation is to develop agreement.

_____ 3. Negotiation is really a lot like a contest between opponents.

_____ 4. Negotiations are head-to-head, no-holds-barred competitions.

_____ 5. In an effective negotiation session, you and the other side work together to arrive at a mutually agreeable resolution.

_____ 6. Negotiations should be win–win situations.

_____ 7. Win–lose negotiations are preferred because the outcome is always clear-cut and definite.

_____ 8. Negotiation generally involves some compromise.

_____ 9. Knowledge or information can help you think creatively in a negotiation.

_____ 10. Time constraints, or deadlines, tend to increase the pressure on negotiators.

_____ 11. In order to reach a viable compromise, the strength (power) in a negotiation must be held by one side.

_____ 12. The side having the most accurate and relevant information will have an advantage during negotiation.

_____ 13. The side with the earliest deadline generally has the weaker position in a negotiation.

_____ 14. Parties in a negotiation will need to perceive a balance of power in order to conclude the negotiations satisfactorily.

Checkpoint 2 Feedback

Check your answers.

1. T
2. T
3. F
4. F
5. T
6. T
7. F
8. T
9. T
10. T
11. F
12. T
13. T
14. T

3 | The Process of Negotiation

This chapter will help you to:

- Explain negotiation as a process rather than an event.
- Describe the negotiation process.
- Identify traits of a successful negotiator.

On the drive home from work that evening, Linda tries to think of some way to manage this vacation conflict. She knows she's got to calm down first, or she'll never get this ironed out with Tom. But negotiations were never her strong suit. Linda has never felt comfortable making deals or swapping favors. "I really want that two-week period," Linda thinks. "I want to avoid a confrontation, but how else can I get to my objective?" ■

THE PROCESS OF NEGOTIATION: A THREE-RING CIRCUS

Negotiation is a process, that, like other processes, has a series of logical steps.

Negotiation is a three-phase process, but the phases are neither as concrete nor as easy as 1-2-3. As you'll soon see, the negotiation process is a lot like a three-ring circus. There's lots of action and everything's happening all at once. The process model illustrates the negotiation process. Refer to it as you read about each phase.

THE NEGOTIATION PROCESS

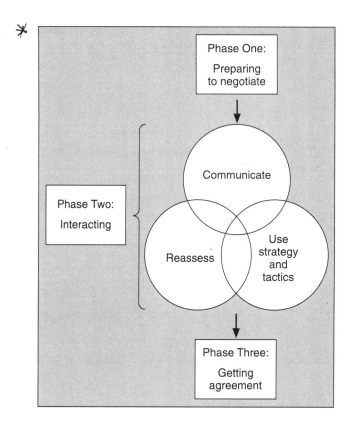

Phase One: Preparing to Negotiate

The first phase of the negotiation process is **preparation**. As you recall from the last chapter, the three critical elements of negotiation—knowledge, power, and deadlines—have a direct and significant impact on the negotiation outcome. Therefore, your preparations will focus on those elements.\In the preparation stage, your primary goal is gathering useful information. At a minimum, you'll spend time analyzing both sides of the conflict. You will determine each side's negotiating objectives or goals. You'll also assess each side's relative knowledge, strength, and deadlines. Finally, you'll determine your own bottom line (stop point), and you'll try to guess the other side's bottom line. Armed with the results of your preparation, you'll move to phase two.

Phase Two: Interacting

The second phase of the process is **interacting**. Here's where the process begins to resemble a three-ring circus. There are three kinds of things that are happening simultaneously within this phase. What's more, in actual negotiating sessions, you'll be jumping back and forth from one ring to another, communicating, applying strategies and tactics, reassessing your position, and then repeating these efforts until you can move toward the close.

3

In this phase you'll work hard at communicating. You begin the negotiating dialogue. The emphasis here is definitely on *dialogue*, a two-way communication. Remember, you are not at the negotiation table to talk. You are not making a speech or delivering a monologue. You should be communicating.

As you communicate in the negotiation process, use three basic skills:

- Active listening.
- Tactful questioning.
- Careful observing.

During this second phase, you'll apply a variety of negotiating *strategies and tactics* to advance the process or gain an advantage that will help you move forward to a positive close. In this phase, the balance of strength/power is apt to shift from one side to another. This changing balance of power will require you to continually probe for more knowledge and constantly reassess your relative position in the negotiation.

You'll also need to *reassess* your position frequently. As new information is uncovered through listening and questioning, as you observe attitudes and body language, and as tactics are tried—you must continuously evaluate three basic options.

- Should you continue negotiating?
- Should you make concessions?
- Should you stand firm?

Now you can see why negotiation skills are in high demand. It takes a great deal of practice to manage all of these various activities. As the negotiation session proceeds, the negotiator must be able to move instantly and smoothly from one set of skills to another—from one ring on the process diagram to another.

Phase Three: Getting Agreement

The third phase of the negotiation process is **getting agreement**. This represents the close of a negotiation session.

You may end or close a negotiation session by getting agreement to resume negotiations at another time. In effect, this is like agreeing to a recess at a trial. You haven't really concluded the negotiations, but for some reason, it's advisable to pause in the effort.

Or, you may end the session because one party has reached its bottom line, the point at which it is not worth the effort to continue negotiating. In this case, you get agreement to abandon the negotiation.

Or, you may close a session by completing the negotiations. In this situation, the negotiated outcome is solidified and details are nailed down. The parties, having cooperated in the give-and-take of compromise, will part with mutual respect.

Hint

The negotiation process varies in length. Some conflicts can be resolved quickly. For instance, you may spend only a minute or two negotiating a restaurant selection for dinner.

In other cases, you may have to allocate hours or days to accommodate several rounds of negotiations. Developing an agreement about all of the elements surrounding your acceptance of a new position at work might require more than one meeting or negotiation session for example.

* TRAITS OF A GOOD NEGOTIATOR

What does it take to be a good negotiator? The successful negotiator has some important characteristics:

1. *Understands people*: A good negotiator understands people. He/she has acquired a practical knowledge of human habits and behaviors, built up over a lifetime of observation and interaction. This understanding seems to be manifest in instinct and intuition. Good negotiators somehow seem to be able to anticipate or guess correctly about the other side's next action or reaction.

2. *Exudes confidence*: There is something very strange about self-confidence. If you don't have it, you can't fake it. If you are not confident, no matter how good an actor you are, you won't really fool the other side for long. On the other hand, if you do have it, it is immediately perceived by the other side. It's almost as if having self-confidence gives the negotiator an aura—the glow of assurance, the expectation of success.

3. *Is open-minded*: If you enter negotiations with a narrow, constricted view, you are probably going to be dissatisfied with the negotiating effort. In order to participate effectively in the give-and take of negotiation, you need to be open-minded. You cannot forge a compromise if you would be unwilling to accept one.

4. *Remains calm*: Negotiations can become emotional. Both sides are subject to losing control over their emotions. It's easy to take a remark personally and respond in haste. It's human nature to get excited, agitated, or irritated with the tone of the conversation or the selection of tactics in a negotiation. The successful negotiator remains calm in the eye of the storm.

5. *Seeks options*: One asset in negotiations is the ability to find or invent alternatives. When a negotiation stalls, with both sides sticking to their predetermined stance, someone must be able to suggest options. Searching for creative alternatives is a trademark of the successful negotiator.

■ Think about It

Do you have what it takes to succeed in negotiations? Complete a personal inventory. Check all of the successful negotiator traits you already have in the list. Then review the ones you didn't check to see where you need to improve.

- ☐ I always observe people carefully.
- ☐ I usually listen more than I talk.
- ☐ I am good at asking questions to elicit information.
- ☐ My questioning style is conversational and friendly.
- ☐ I am good at guessing how people will react to my ideas.
- ☐ I can frequently predict what the other side will say or do next in a negotiation.
- ☐ I control my emotions even when attacked personally in a negotiation.
- ☐ Self-confidence comes naturally to me.
- ☐ I listen attentively.
- ☐ I like solving problems.
- ☐ I would rather work with other people than work alone.
- ☐ Conflict does not scare me.
- ☐ I am a patient person.
- ☐ I am thoughtful and logical.
- ☐ I enjoy selecting from alternatives.
- ☐ I usually look at all the options before I make a decision.
- ☐ The win–win concept fits in with my philosophy of life.

Chapter 3 Checkpoints

1. Describe each phase of the negotiation process in your own words, then review the process diagram in this chapter.

Phase One:

_____

_____

_____

_____

_____

Phase Two:

a. _____

_____

_____

b. _____

_____

_____

c. _____

_____

_____

_____

Phase Three:

_____

_____

_____

_____

_____

2. Someone once observed that people tend to become better negotiators as they get older. Do you agree? Why or why not?

_____

_____

_____

Checkpoint 3 Feedback

Check your answers. Allow for reasonable variations.

Phase One: Preparing to negotiate.

The goal is gathering information that may be useful during negotiation. You will analyze both sides of the conflict, identify goals, and assess each side's opening position.

Phase Two: Interacting.

This is the heart of the negotiation—an interactive dialogue between parties. You will:

    a. Communicate.
    b. Use various negotiating strategies and tactics.
    c. Constantly reassess your position.

Phase Three: Getting agreement.

This is the close of the negotiation. You agree to continue the negotiation, abandon the negotiation, or you reach a mutually satisfactory agreement.

CHAPTER

4 | Preparing for Negotiation

This chapter will help you to:

- Prepare for a negotiation.
- Analyze the objectives, motives, or needs of both sides.
- Assess the starting positions of both sides.
- Define the bottom line position for both sides.

Across town, Tom is fixing dinner and making plans. He's irritated that his manager passed the buck on the vacation conflict. He'd just as soon avoid facing Linda on this issue, since she's been talking about her class reunion for weeks. But he's booked and paid for a cruise vacation. "So, now what do I do?" Tom wonders. "If only I knew what Linda was thinking right now . . ." ■

THE VALUE OF PREPARATION

In the last chapter, we reviewed the negotiating process and compared it to a three-ring circus. No wonder most people feel a bit insecure as they approach a negotiating session. There is a lot of pressure to perform. The other side is analyzing your every move. Your mistakes will be noticed. There may be many people affected by the outcome of your negotiating efforts. What's more, you've got to think, act, and react in real time. So many things are happening at once during the negotiation session that you begin to feel a bit like a juggler trying desperately to keep things flowing smoothly without missing a beat.

Now imagine if you lacked confidence. You are not really sure of your skills. You doubt your ability to pull it off. The tension grows as the negotiation session approaches. Negotiation can be a major source of stress.

How can you control this runaway locomotive called anxiety? The answer is preparation.

The best way to reduce anxiety about a negotiation is to prepare for it. Careful deliberation and thoughtful consideration will reduce your anxiety, build your confidence, and increase the likelihood of your success.

Preparing for Negotiations

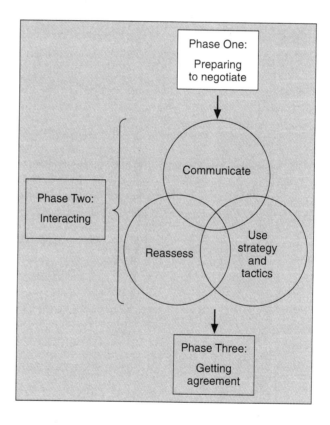

What's involved in preparing to negotiate? Your first goal is gathering information that will enable you to:

- Identify your side's motives, objectives, or needs and then make an educated guess about the other side's.
- Assess your own starting position, then do the same for the other side.

- Define your side's bottom line and attempt to define the other side's bottom line.

Take a closer look at each of these three areas of preparation.

Identifying Motives, Objectives, or Needs

To assess motives, objectives, or needs, ask yourself these questions:

- What do you hope to achieve as a result of the negotiation effort?
- What are your primary needs? Secondary needs?
- Why are you engaging in this negotiation?
- Are you a willing player or a forced participant?
- What is at risk in the negotiation?
- What do you want to get?

Give these questions some careful thought. As you work through the preparation phase of negotiations, you may need to ask these questions at two levels.

In some negotiations, you'll be negotiating just for yourself, one-on-one with another party. For instance, you might be negotiating with your neighbor over where the property line is for a new fence he's building. In that case, you'll be asking yourself these questions and then asking and answering them for your neighbor. The answers to your questions will be at only one level.

In other situations, you'll be negotiating on behalf of another entity—your company, a club, a task force or committee, and so on. For example, as chairperson of the banquet planning committee for your local charity, you may be negotiating with several hotels as potential locations for the event. In this situation, you must ask these questions at two levels, personal and representative.

Why two levels? Because the negotiation is being done by you for another party. You may be perfectly willing to spend $50 for a charity dinner event, but your committee may have set a maximum of $30. So your objectives and needs—at the two levels—may not always be the same. The same is true of the other side. The hotel salesperson may have a personal need to assist your charitable organization by obtaining the best price for you, but he or she also has an obligation as a representative of the hotel to maximize profit on the hotel's services. If this negotiation is to succeed, you'll need to understand needs and objectives at both levels.

Assessing the Starting Positions

In order to develop an effective negotiating strategy or plan your negotiating tactics, assess the starting position for yourself and the other side. Estimate your relative positions with regard to the three critical elements: information/knowledge, power/strength, and time or deadline pressure.

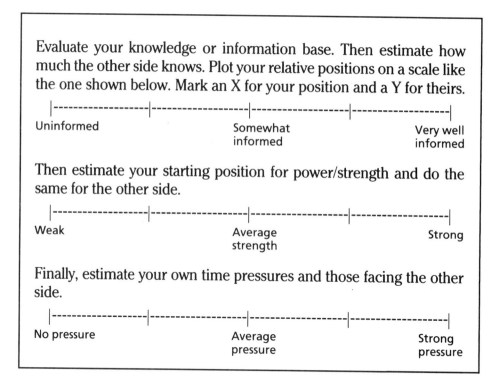

When you've analyzed the three critical elements and marked the corresponding scales, take a few moments to reflect on your results. Look at your side's relative position on each scale. Who appears to have the more advantageous opening position?

1. If you have the opening advantage, ask yourself these questions:
   a. What information do I still need to know? How will I get it?
   b. How can I maintain my advantage in perceived strength? or How can we get closer to a balance of power?

   c. What can I do to ease my time pressures or increase time pressures on the other side?

2. If the other side has the opening advantage, ask yourself these questions:

   a. What do I still need to know? How will I uncover missing information? How can I minimize information going to the other side?

   b. What steps might I take to balance power in the negotiation? Are there any ways of gaining power for my side or removing it from the other side?

   c. How can I offset my deadline pressure? How can I increase pressure on the other side?

Establishing the Bottom Line

In every negotiable situation, there is a point of no return. You need to decide on your bottom line. Then make an educated guess as to the other party's bottom line. Consider an example to see how this works.

Imagine that you are negotiating with another department in your company to get print materials ready for distribution to your customers. You have determined that if your internal resources charge more than $5,000 or take longer than two weeks to get the job done, then you are ready to walk away from the negotiation and do business with an outside vendor.

You've got to guess what that department's bottom line is. Perhaps they've set a bottom line based on time alone. You suspect that they are already overbooked, and that they'll be unable to turn your job around within the two-week time frame. However, you think they'll come in well under your price ceiling. Is negotiation feasible? Of course.

When you have estimated each side's bottom line you are in a much better position to come up with potential alternatives or options. For the situation we just described, what would you be willing to offer in order to get your job done in the two-week time frame? (Write your ideas below.)

_____

_____

You could offer to offset their schedule problems by paying a premium price to cover overtime on the job, providing it doesn't exceed your bottom line maximum of $5,000. Thinking about the bottom lines can point you to logical options for mutual problem solving.

Hint

Remember the Boy Scout motto? *Be prepared.* It's excellent advice for anyone approaching a negotiating session.

Think about It

Consider one of your own recent negotiation experiences, and answer the following questions.

1. Were you worried about the outcome of the negotiation?

_____

2. How much time did you spend in preparing for negotiation?

_____

3. What did you actually do to prepare?

_____
_____
_____
_____

5. Did you assess needs/motives? _____
Did you assess positions on the three critical elements? _____
Did you consider bottom lines? _____

4. What was the outcome of the negotiation?

_____
_____

5. As you look back on the situation, were you adequately prepared?

_____

6. What would you do differently if you were just beginning your preparations now?

_____
_____
_____
_____

Use the planning worksheet to prepare for your next negotiating session.

NEGOTIATION PLANNING WORKSHEET

Identify motives, objectives, needs:

- What do you hope to achieve as a result of the negotiation effort?

- What are your primary needs? Secondary needs?

- Why are you engaging in this negotiation?

- Are you a willing player or a forced participant?

- What is at risk in the negotiation?

- What do you want to get?

Assess starting positions:

- Which side has the advantage in terms of knowledge or information?

- Which side has the advantage in relative strength or power?

- Which side has the advantage in time pressures or deadlines?

Calculate the bottom line:

- At what point are you prepared to abandon the negotiation?

- At what point do you feel the other side will walk away from the negotiation?

4

Chapter 4 Checkpoints

Mark each statement T or F.

_____ 1. Preparation is the first phase in the negotiating process.

_____ 2. Most people are not intimidated by the prospect of a negotiation session.

_____ 3. Negotiation sessions are linear events—things happen one step at a time moving in a straight line toward a resolution.

_____ 4. Preparation will not help dispel negotiation anxiety.

_____ 5. Sometimes you will be assessing needs and motives at two levels, personal and representative.

_____ 6. Your starting position in a negotiation will depend on how you compare to the other side in terms of knowledge, strength, and deadline pressure.

_____ 7. You would use the same negotiating strategy whether you had the opening advantage or not.

_____ 8. In the context of negotiation, the _bottom line_ means the point at which you're ready to give up on the negotiation.

_____ 9. Most of the work in preparation involves gathering information and analyzing it.

_____ 10. Knowing the other side's bottom line can help you think up options and alternatives to arrive at mutually agreeable solutions.

What three tasks should you undertake to prepare for negotiations?

_____

_____

_____

Checkpoint 4 Feedback

 Check your answers with those provided below.

1. T
2. F
3. F
4. F
5. T
6. T
7. F
8. T
9. T
10. T

The three tasks are:

1. Identify the motives, objectives, or needs for both your side and the other side.
2. Assess starting positions relative to the three critical elements.
3. Define your bottom line and estimate that of the other side.

5 | Using Communication Skills in Negotiation

This chapter will help you to:

- Ask useful questions in a negotiation session.
- Listen actively during a negotiation session.
- Carefully observe the other side during negotiations.

"There's no time like the present," Linda thinks as she sits down to open the morning mail at work. "I've got to take some action to get this vacation issue settled. But what'll I say? What'll Tom ask me? How can I get past the hostile look on his face? How am I ever going to get to that reunion?"

"This isn't going to be easy," Tom reflects as he sips coffee at his desk. "What is Linda going to suggest? What ideas am I prepared to offer? How are we going to get this thing behind us and still stay friends at work?" ∎

MOVING INTO PHASE TWO OF THE NEGOTIATION PROCESS

In the last chapter, you focused on Phase One of the negotiation process—getting ready for negotiations. In this chapter, we're moving into the second phase of the negotiation process, interacting. A critical element in interacting is communication.

When you are actively engaged in the negotiation dialogue, you'll be using three primary communication skills:

- Tactful questioning.
- Active listening.
- Careful observation.

Let's see how each of these communication skills fits into the context of negotiation.

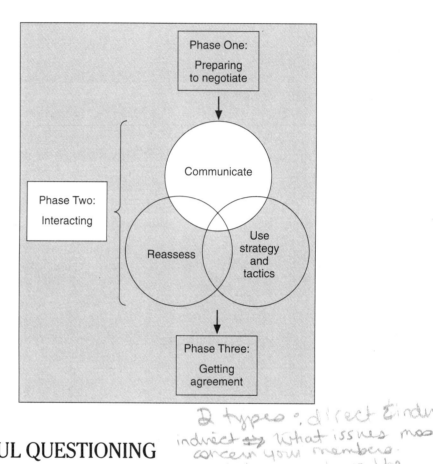

TACTFUL QUESTIONING

[handwritten margin note: 2 types: direct & indirect
indirect ⇒ What issues most concern your members.
direct ⇒ Do you have the authority to decide this matter]

As you prepared for negotiation, you asked and answered a lot of questions. That questioning process, once begun, becomes a constant feature of the negotiating process. Stripped of its mystique, a negotiation is simply a dialogue or conversation that involves the asking and answering of questions. Astute questioning uncovers information that may enable you to complete the negotiation successfully. That's why your questioning skills become critical for successful negotiations.

Types of Questions

You'll have many opportunities to ask questions during an average negotiation session. But a word of caution is in order: Be sure that you frame your questions carefully and ask them intentionally.

Two types of questions are most frequently used during negotiations: direct and indirect. Take a brief look at each of them.

Imagine that you wanted to find out more about the other side's needs. You'd want to ask questions that encourage the other side to open up, to explain, to give you additional background information willingly. Questions that encourage wider-ranging responses are *indirect questions*. Here are some examples of indirect questions:

- Why are you interested in obtaining more time to decide?
- How is your negotiating team organized?
- What are you hoping to achieve during this negotiating session?
- What issues most concern your members?
- Can you explain how you arrived at that position?

In other cases, you simply want to uncover facts or move the dialogue along. You are looking for brief, clear answers. For these situations, you'd choose *direct questions*. Here are some examples of direct questions:

- Will we be able to complete our session by noon today?
- Can we agree to meet again tomorrow?
- Do you prefer the 60-day or 90-day implementation plan?
- Do you have authority to decide this matter?
- Is the corporate benefits package confirmed with your team?
- Are we in agreement on the terms of the deal?

Your challenge in negotiations is to know when and how to use the two types of questions effectively. Focus on the basic intent of each of your questions. If you are seeking specific information or trying to verify information, use direct questions. If you are trying to uncover problems, determine needs, or understand issues, use indirect questions.

5

Framing Questions

There is more to questioning than simply asking direct or indirect questions. The same question may be framed in a number of ways, and each variation will produce a different effect. Suppose you need to find out why workers did not get overtime pay. Read each of the following questions and think about the effect it might have when asked in a negotiation.

1. "What's your excuse for not paying overtime to the workers?"
2. "How come you didn't pay the required overtime?"
3. "Would you help us understand why you were unable to pay the overtime?"
4. "There seems to be a misunderstanding, so will you explain how overtime pay is calculated?

Each question is aimed at finding out the same kind of information, but the questions are phrased in ways that range from openly hostile (1) to conciliatory (4). Can you see that the other side will respond differently to each form of the question? Take pains to frame your questions carefully.

When framing questions to ask during negotiations, you need to consider:

- What information do you want to uncover?
- What kind of question (direct or indirect) is most likely to elicit the information you need?
- What kind of effect (positive, negative, neutral) do you want the question to have on the other side?
- What tone or emotional impact (aggressive, passive, hostile, conciliatory, etc.) do you want to make with the question?

Think about It

Try writing questions that are intended to produce a certain effect. If you are facing an upcoming negotiation, use it in this exercise. If not, use the examples.

Imagine that you are negotiating with your manager about your workload. You want to find out how many accounts the other service people have. You believe that you have been handling many more accounts than the others, and you are earning the same wages as they are.

1. Write a direct question with a neutral tone.

_____

_____

2. Rewrite the question with an aggressive or threatening tone.

_____

_____

3. Revise the question to give it a friendly or conciliatory tone.

_____

_____

4. Write an indirect question to get the other side talking in general on the topic.

_____

_____

Imagine you are negotiating to buy a used computer. You think the asking price is too high based on your estimate of the original price. You'd like to know what the original price really was and the age of the computer.

1. Write a direct question with a neutral tone.

_____

_____

2. Write an indirect question.

_____

_____

ACTIVE LISTENING

If questioning is one key skill in negotiation, you've probably already figured out that listening is another. Because negotiation is a dialogue—a two-way exchange of information—you're going to spend a good portion of your negotiating time listening to what the other party says.

5

Active listening implies more than simply hearing what the other party says. When you listen actively, you are thinking, analyzing, and considering the other side's comments or questions. You are paying close attention to what is said. You are focused and energized. You are examining the words, the tone of voice, the choice of phrases. You are attuned to the spoken nuances that may reveal attitudes and opinions or shed light on the other side's needs and concerns.

The biggest source of mistakes in negotiations is failing to listen. When you do not listen carefully, you are likely to:

- Misinterpret what the other side said.
- Be unable to confirm or verify what was said.
- Misunderstand the other side's question.
- Make improper assumptions.
- Be unable to respond appropriately.
- Confuse the situation.
- Slow the progress of negotiations.
- Select the wrong strategies or tactics to advance the negotiation.

Listen carefully, as though the outcome of the negotiation depended upon it—because it does.

CAREFUL OBSERVATION

Your listening and questioning skills are important factors in managing verbal communications in a negotiating session. But you also need to consider another level—nonverbal communication.

Nonverbal communication involves visible movements or gestures that convey emotions or intentions. For example, when you frown and fold your arms as you speak to a child, you are clearly communicating your displeasure via nonverbal means. When you smile and move closer to another person, you are communicating your comfort, approval, or interest.

How do you know what a gesture or expression means? By the time you reach adulthood, you have amassed many years of experience in observing physical movements and gestures. By trial and error, you've become attuned to the probable meaning associated with a slumping posture or a weak handshake—you've learned through life's experience. Now you've got to apply that knowledge in the negotiating session.

Your Powers of Observation

Use your powers of observation to learn more about the other party's feelings and emotions. What you see during the negotiation session may be just as important as what you hear.

- Watch for changes in facial expression that may be clues to changing moods or may reveal reactions to something you have proposed or suggested.
- Watch for hand gestures or mannerisms that may offer clues to state of mind or emotional level.
- Watch for physical movements or changing positions in the room that may hint at the other side's thinking or reveal their perceptions of the negotiating situation.

Studied Reactions and Cultural Differences

Sometimes your observations are subject to interpretation. A masterful negotiator, for instance, may have acquired the ability to mask or disguise feelings by adopting a pose of indifference. This practiced act may prevent you from observing the real emotional response to a negotiating tactic. It can be difficult to know, for certain, if the other party is really indifferent to

5

an idea or only seem indifferent. As a rule, very few people are able to consistently hide their reactions. A shrewd observer would probably detect small breaks in the surface perfection of these studied reactions. Of course, veteran negotiators will often be harder to read than beginners.

Cultural differences can also add to the complexity of observing and interpreting nonverbal communications. In Latin American countries, people stand close to each other in discussion. In the United States, people tend to stand a bit farther apart in conversation. Thus, you may need to factor in culture when you attempt to interpret the other side's tendency to lean toward you at every opportunity.

Also, in some cultures such as ours, time is a pressing issue, but in some other cultures, a deadline is not taken seriously. The importance placed on timeliness, time pressure, or deadline will vary substantially from one culture to another.

Are you aware of other cultural, social, or linguistic differences that could impact your ability to communicate in upcoming negotiations? Jot down some examples of cultural differences that you have observed or that you expect to encounter in future negotiations.

_____

_____

_____

Hint

Unintentional sounds are also clues to the other side's state of mind. For example, many people reveal their nervousness through shallow coughing or continually clearing the throat. Others may show their tension by a tendency to laugh or giggle nervously.

Chapter 5 Checkpoints

Test your own powers of observation. For each nonverbal communication item described, write in your interpretation. Assume that you are in a negotiation session and are observing these reactions.

1. Staring in silence.

_____

2. Leaning forward across the table.

_____

3. Blushing.

_____

4. Tapping a pencil on the table.

_____

5. Looking out the window.

_____

6. Blank expression, or poker face.

_____

7. Jaw clenching.

_____

8. Excessive hand gestures or movements.

_____

9. Sitting across from you rather than beside you.

_____

10. Maintaining eye contact with you when you speak.

_____

11. Getting up from the table and moving around the room.

_____

12. Blinking very frequently.

_____

Checkpoint 5 Feedback

Check your responses. Remember that some of these nonverbal conditions may have more than one potential interpretation.

1. Anger or agitation (making a studied effort not to react).
2. Interest, commitment, or curiosity.
3. Embarrassment, anger, or aggression.
4. Nervousness, anxiety, or impatience.
5. Boredom, disenchantment, disinterest, or lack of concentration.
6. An emotional reaction that is intentionally stifled.
7. Aggravation, irritation, or impatience.
8. Agitation, tension, or nervousness.
9. Hostility, opposition, or egotism.
10. Interest, candor, or concurrence.
11. Agitation or feeling trapped, tense, or frustrated.
12. Anger, excitement, or frustration.

CHAPTER

6 | Using Negotiation Techniques

This chapter will help you to:

- Apply negotiation techniques and tactics to advance the negotiation process.
- Respond appropriately when the other side uses proven negotiation techniques and tactics during a negotiation session.

Tom and Linda have managed to avoid each other for the better part of an hour at work. Finally, Linda calls Tom to suggest they have lunch and work out a resolution to their vacation conflict. Tom immediately accepts. As they hang up the phone, both are on the same emotional plateau, thinking that time's running out. The negotiations are about to begin. ■

MOVING FORWARD IN THE NEGOTIATION PROCESS

You concentrated on communications skills in the last chapter. Now let's move on to another of the three rings in Phase Two of the negotiation process—applying negotiating strategies and tactics.

In the broadest sense, a negotiating strategy is a general approach or method that you plan to apply during the session. A tactic, on the other hand, is a more specific technique or action that you plan to use to execute your strategy.

You might adopt a general strategy that is aggressive or confrontational. In that case, you'd select tactics that would be appropriate for that approach. In another case, you might select a cooperative or consensus-building strategy, so you'd have to select tactics that are in line with that

51

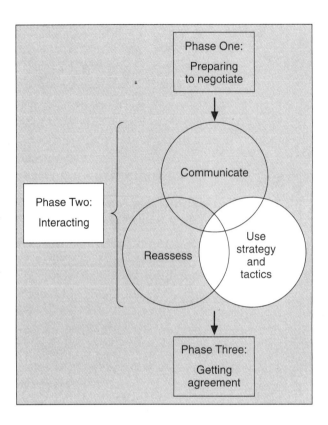

approach. Incidentally, once you've selected a general strategy, you are not necessarily bound to it for the duration of the negotiation. You may change strategies and tactics at any time in a negotiation.

During the actual negotiation session, you will be constantly evaluating your position and that of the other side. Using information and insights you obtain by listening, questioning, and observation, you quickly select or modify your negotiating strategies and tactics. Your guiding objective is to move the negotiation process forward to Phase Three, getting agreement.

In this chapter, the focus is on the negotiating session itself. You're going to learn about a variety of proven negotiating techniques. Depending on your level of experience in negotiation, some of the techniques may be familiar. Others may be new to you.

> **Hint**
>
> Before the negotiating techniques, a word of caution is in order. The techniques represent the real world of negotiating. However, people vary in their sense of what is right or fair in negotiation. Therefore, some techniques may seem OK to you, while others may seem sneaky or manipulative. You decide which techniques you'd like to try. Bear in mind that the other side may try these techniques against you, so you need to be aware of them, even if you wouldn't choose to use them yourself.

COMMON NEGOTIATING TECHNIQUES

Experienced negotiators will have a wide range of strategies and tactics at their disposal. Our exploration of this topic will begin by reviewing some common negotiating techniques.

Stonewalling

As you already know, time pressures or deadlines represent one of the three critical elements in any negotiation.

Suppose you are under severe deadline pressure to conclude the negotiation. The other side seems to be doing everything except negotiating. They are asking for delays and postponements. They are providing excuses for not attending prearranged meetings. They are starting late and leaving early. They are losing track of their paperwork, calling the home office, waiting to hear from someone about something. Meanwhile, your frustration builds until you are just about to blow up and lose control over the negotiation process. This is not an accidental series of events. This is a strategy called *stonewalling*.

The idea here is to stall and delay, causing the other side to become short-tempered and agitated as its deadline looms closer. The classic example of this is the filibuster used in the U.S. Senate. Senators keep talking to delay dealing with outstanding issues and postpone voting on a touchy point.

There are many instances when this kind of approach is used in daily and work life. Can you think of some negotiating situations where this approach has been used on you? Have you stonewalled someone?

_____

_____

_____

_____

_____

The operative issue in stonewalling is time. When one of the parties in a negotiation uses this approach, he/she is really saying: "I can last longer than you can." Stonewalling may be apparent at the outset of a negotiation, or it may suddenly appear at some point after negotiations are underway. Whenever you encounter it, you need to be prepared to respond.

How will you respond to stonewalling? The first thing you need to do is identify it. This is important, though seemingly obvious. Once you identify the strategy, you immediately minimize its effectiveness. You can step back, and say to yourself: "I see where the other side is headed. They are not going to drag me down that road kicking and screaming in frustration."

Then you are in a position to respond with a more suitable, less emotional reaction. One response is to fight fire with fire. Get your own deadline extended to take the pressure off. Then wait patiently for the other side to make a move. Another response attempts to increase the deadline pressure for the other side. You may be able to find out more about their own time pressures and use that information to advantage.

A third approach might be to turn the other side's strategy back on them. Let them know that you are relieved that the pace of negotiations seems to have slowed or stopped. Indicate your preference for a slower time schedule; describe how busy you are with other commitments or more pressing issues. In short, put the ball back into their court.

What other tactics might work when you face a negotiator who is stonewalling you? _____

_____

_____

_____

_____

> ### Hint
>
> People have different thresholds for frustration and delay. Some people are not bothered by delaying tactics. Others are quick to lose their intellectual focus when delaying tactics are employed.
>
> Do you hate waiting in lines? Are you irritated by airline schedule problems? Do you resent wasting time? If so, you need to be on the alert for delaying tactics because they will provoke you into making poor negotiating choices. In negotiations, you really must know yourself and your reactions, so they will not be used against you.

Impulsive Change

Change can often be unsettling, especially when the change is unexpected. (Suppose you are negotiating smoothly and methodically. Both sides are working seriously and steadfastly to move the negotiation process forward. Suddenly, with no apparent reason, the other side becomes irrational on one issue.)

How do you feel when this happens? You're probably surprised and somewhat confused by the change in behavior. If you're not careful, you'll discover yourself conceding the issue before you know it. What's happening? It's an approach called the *impulsive change*. The sudden shift in attitude or emotion draws attention to itself. Just when you thought everything was working well, without warning the other side makes a dramatic shift in attitude, approach, or tactics. (They hope to upset your equilibrium, to draw attention to an issue, or simply to shake up what they perceive as complacency.)

How have you used the impulsive change approach? Has anyone tried it on you? Was it successful?

_____
_____
_____
_____
_____

To respond effectively to an impulsive change by the other side, you need to think fast. What motives lie behind the change? Can the sudden change be explained rationally? Or does it seem totally out of context? If you cannot answer these questions to your own satisfaction, then you need to ask the other side. What provoked the change? Encourage your opponent to interpret, rationalize, or otherwise explain the change.

Assuming you understand the motivation behind the change, you may adopt other tactics. For example, you may choose to ignore the sudden change. If the intent is to surprise you or catch you off guard, then a lack of surprise on your part will be disarming for the other side. Another approach might be simply to acknowledge the use of the tactic, then give in without a fuss if this issue is a deal-breaker. But remind the other side that the tactic will only work once.

What other tactics might be appropriate to use when the other side makes an impulsive change?

_____
_____
_____
_____
_____

The Gotcha

A *gotcha* is an approach used by people who prefer to act now and negotiate later. A gotcha forces the issue being negotiated. This approach has some serious risks, but it can be effective if used judiciously.

Let's look an example. Imagine that you are about to negotiate the family vacation, an arduous process of listening to diverse views and trying to make everyone happy. You might decide to take the initiative, make reservations at an amusement center, and then start negotiating. What's the advantage here? Well, you could probably manage the negotiations to steer family members toward your foregone conclusion—the amusement park vacation. Or you can simply announce that the destination is chosen, but other factors are negotiable—such as how long to stay, where to stay, etc. The disadvantage of this approach should be obvious. The other parties may feel manipulated, especially if they would rather have gone, say, to the beach or on a camp trip to the mountains.

Consider a business application of the gotcha approach. Suppose you are part of a quality team that is developing a package of fringe benefits for workers. Your team is developing minimum requirements in health insurance, dental care, and eye exams, then you'll negotiate with management to get these benefits instituted. Your side is centered on keeping and increasing benefits, not reducing them. The management group has taken the opposite stand, cutting fringe benefits. After several sessions in which little progress was made, management selects a provider without further consultation with the quality team. At the next negotiating session, they present the provider who will now be part of their negotiating team.

What can you do? You are facing a gotcha at its best. A single act has forced the issue, restructured the negotiating team, severely limited the scope of feasible options for agreement, and irrevocably altered the negotiation atmosphere. Negotiations now will focus only on the variations this provider offers.

This negotiating technique works best when power is unevenly distributed at the negotiating table. It is thus often associated with negotiators who are accustomed to top-down management styles.

Have you ever used this approach? What risks did you take? Did it work? Does this tactic work against you?

_____
_____
_____
_____
_____

How would you feel if this approach were used on you? Do you approve of this kind of tactic?

_____
_____
_____
_____
_____

The Dodge

The *dodge* technique is one of the oldest and most effective. The conventional dodge uses a ploy to shift attention from the real issue to a side issue like a skillful pickpocket distracting the intended victim with a push or bump while taking the wallet or watch. A negotiator might launch into a side topic—a diversion—to distract attention from the real objective.

Here's a business example. You are trying to recruit and hire a division manager. One of your objectives is to get a three-year commitment. You are not really concerned about the wage/fringe package. Nevertheless, you may choose to focus the discussion on wage/fringe issues in order to divert attention from the long-term commitment you must obtain. Then when you get to an agreement on wages and benefits, you'll suggest and insist on the three-year idea.

Another variation on this theme is "testing the waters." In this form of the dodge, you'd casually mention an idea early in the negotiation and see how the other side responds to it. You position your idea as a trial balloon, just something to kick around and explore, not an idea to which you are committed.

Then you abandon the idea for a while, but you'll return to it near the end of the negotiation when you have figured out a strategy and a set of tactics that will enable you to gain agreement on that original idea.

The dodge is really an attempt to avoid talking about an issue or need head on. It is not a direct move to satisfy needs in a negotiation session; rather, it is an oblique route to obtain what you want.

How can you respond when this technique is tried on you? First, listen carefully for seemingly casual remarks or suggestions. Be cognizant of the other side's attempts to test the waters or float a trial balloon. See through the facade of the dodge. Focus on the other side's real interests and needs. When the other side veers off on a tangential discussion, bring them back gently but firmly to the current issue. Redirect attention to the agreed-upon agenda or refocus on the matter at hand. Or if you prefer, make a mental note of the dodge, and let the other side continue with it. Of course, you are preparing, in the meantime, to counter it with a strategy or tactic of your own choosing.

Have you had experience with this strategy? How would you respond to the other side's attempts to use the dodge?

_____
_____
_____
_____
_____

Might you choose and apply this technique in negotiation? What are the risks of failure?

_____
_____
_____
_____
_____

6

■ **Think about It**

You've just read about several negotiation strategies or techniques. Take a moment to reflect on the use of them.

1. Check the strategies you'd feel comfortable using in a negotiation.

☐ Stonewalling.
☐ Impulsive change.
☐ The gotcha.
☐ The dodge.

2. For the items you didn't check above, what makes you uncomfortable with them?

_____
_____
_____
_____
_____
_____
_____

A rock-and-roll song suggests "different strokes for different folks." You need not use a given strategy or tactic, but you do need to be aware of them, so you can respond effectively when they are used on you.

3. Which of the strategies we've covered so far appear to be more useful for win–win negotiations? Why?

_____

_____

_____

_____

_____

SELECTED NEGOTIATING TACTICS

We've just looked at some of the broader approaches to negotiating. Let's turn our attention to some specific negotiating tactics that you'll be likely to encounter in a business negotiating session.

High Ball/Low Ball

Everyone has had some experience with the high-ball/low-ball tactic. Here's how it works. If you are the seller in a negotiation, you might choose to start out with a *high-ball* price—a sales price that is very high, much higher than you really expect to receive. In the United States, for example, everyone knows that the sticker price posted on new cars is not the real price. It's more like an asking price. Similarly, manufacturers often tag their merchandise with an artificially high price called the manufacturer's suggested retail price. Again, that high-ball price allows retailers to offer consumers a supposed discount off the suggested price. If you decided to sell your house, you probably advertised an inflated price, fully expecting to settle for something less. This high-ball approach to negotiation is very widespread.

Similarly, if you are the buyer, you will probably begin negotiations with a *low-ball* figure—a price too low. You expect to end up paying more than your original offer, but you've chosen to use the low-ball tactic.

Psychologically, the high-ball/low-ball approach is intended to make both parties feel as if they are winners in the pricing game. They will gradually inch toward a central price somewhere between the high ball and the low ball. This gradual concession in price makes each party feel in control of the bargaining situation. The dialogue will go something like this:

Joe:

> These computers are priced at $1,200 per unit. Peripherals are extra. [High-ball price.]

Bob:

> Well, I've got a limited budget. We need 12 units, but can only pay $800 per unit. [Low-ball price.]

Joe:

> Well, you are a good customer, and we value your business. We may be able to let them go at $1,100 apiece.

Bob:

> That's more like it, but we're still pretty far apart. I'm willing to come up a little if you'll come down a bit.

Joe:

> "Bob, you drive a hard bargain. If I give you a price of $1,000 per unit, will you buy 12 of them right now?"

Bob:

> "That seems fair. Let's agree on $1,000 each." [Real price.]

The pattern of high ball and low ball has become so prevalent that it approaches the level of ritual. You may encounter some seasoned negotiators who simply feel they must dance through this pricing scenario every time around. On the other hand, since this tactic has become so prevalent, it has really lost most of its effectiveness. Some new-breed negotiators would prefer to cut right to the real figures and save the ritual. Your challenge in negotiation is to know when to play the numbers game and when to get right to the heart of the matter.

An Emotional Outburst

Most business negotiations tend to be calm and orderly. But once in a while, an emotional outburst can be an effective tactic. An emotional display can intimidate, embarrass, or otherwise befuddle the other side. The effects may not last long, but they can be powerful.

Assume you are negotiating with an employee to gain agreement to a demotion—a lesser-paying position within your department. Everything's going well until the employee bursts into tears about the impossibility of making ends meet on that pay. If you're an average person, your negotiations have just been undermined by an emotional outburst. Whether the outburst was carefully calculated or entirely spontaneous and genuine, the outcome is the same. You couldn't possibly rationalize less pay to some-one who is obviously so distressed at the notion. Even though your negoti-ation plan was carefully prepared and your rationalizations for the pay cut were perfectly businesslike, that all goes out the window when an outburst occurs.

Now imagine yourself at the negotiating table working out the division of sales territories. When you get to the allocation for salespeople in the western region, suddenly the sales manager jumps up, bangs a fist on the table, and yells: "No way. I'm not settling for that. You're trying to make our region look inferior to the eastern region. I'm not putting up with it." Everyone looks sheepishly toward you. What are you going to do? How can you respond to the emotional outburst?

It's not easy to remain calm, but, in fact, that's exactly what you have to do. Try to retain your composure. Don't rush into apologies or sympathies. If necessary, call a time out to let the other person cool off. When the immediate crisis has passed, you might try to discuss the situation, explor-ing what provoked the outburst or examining how you might work together to get over the emotional hurdle.

There are many variations on the theme of the emotional outburst. How many of the following emotional outbursts have you experienced in the context of a negotiation?

- ☐ Mild threats.
- ☐ Uncontrollable laughter.
- ☐ The silent treatment.
- ☐ Leaving the session with no explanation.
- ☐ Pounding the table.
- ☐ Yelling or shouting.
- ☐ Crying.
- ☐ Threatening retaliation.
- ☐ Making you feel guilty.
- ☐ Intimidating you with force or power.

The Ebenezer Scrooge Tactic

Ebenezer Scrooge was a miserly, very tight-fisted fellow. Getting a dime out of Scrooge was like trying to wring liquid from a stone. Many would-be negotiators think Ebenezer Scrooge is the patron saint of negotiation, and they prefer his miserly approach to concessions during negotiation.

In win–win negotiations, the process is clearly one of give-and-take. The average person thinks that the increments of concession should be about equal. In our earlier dialogue example about computer prices, for instance, the approximate size of the price concession was equal on both sides. If we are ready to compromise, we expect the other side to do the same. If we are ready to make concessions, we expect a concession of equal weight or value in return.

In contrast, some negotiators insist on using the Scrooge approach. They are all take and no give, or they resist giving until the very last possible moment. These highly competitive negotiators will take pride in forcing you to give in first, manipulating you into giving up more than they do, and pressuring you to settle for less than they do.

The Scrooge tactic can be effective if you are intimidated by this kind of power play. However, if you have carefully prepared for negotiation and developed a minimal bottom line, then you will not be fooled by this tactic. After all, you don't really care who gives in first or who appears to get more. You have clearly defined needs to meet and a bottom line to tell you when to close out your efforts.

To combat this tactic, try a direct approach. (Suggest that you expect a shared give and take with mutual concession leading to a negotiated agreement. Confirm that the other side shares this attitude.) Probe with questions to find out if the other side really wants to move forward with negotiation or whether they are just wasting time playing power games.

A second response to the Scrooge tactic is to acknowledge it outright. Say something like, "It seems you are hung up on who gives in first." It's doubtful they'll choose to pursue the tactic any further after it's out in the open.

Have you had any negotiation experiences where the other side acted like Scrooge? What did you do? Were you able to reach a mutually agreeable, win-win solution?

_____
_____
_____
_____

Mother-May-I

There is nothing more frustrating than trying to negotiate with someone who doesn't have the authority to make decisions. Does this sound familiar?

You:

So, we've agreed that you'll provide all the artwork for manuals, right?

Manager:

Yes, but . . . I'll have to verify that with the graphics group.

You:

> And we've agreed that the project will be completed by August 1, providing your subject matter experts are available this week.

Manager:

> Yes, but . . . I have to get permission from the department managers involved so we can tap the experts.

You:

> Well, we've agreed the book will be no more than 100 pages and you're going to pay me a fixed price of $25,000. Right?

Manager:

> Yes, but . . . the experts may think we need more text pages. Of course, I'll have to get permission from purchasing and an authorized signature from my manager to spend more than $10,000.

At this point you're probably wondering whether you're negotiating with the right person. This manager doesn't seem to have authority to make any kind of decision or commitment. That might be simple reality at this company, but it may be the mother-may-I tactic at work.

In the mother-may-I tactic, the other party insists he or she has limited authority to make any commitments. Indeed, this tactic buys time, slowing the pace of negotiation. If it's true, then you may be in for a very long and frustrating negotiation. To combat this strategy, you might want to suggest that the decision maker be present for future negotiation sessions. If it's a ploy, then the other side is using a stonewalling strategy to delay action.

What other tactics could you use to combat the mother-may-I approach?

_____

_____

_____

_____

Use the planning worksheet on page 66 to help select strategies and tactics for your next negotiating session.

6

NEGOTIATION STRATEGY AND TACTICS WORKSHEET

Identify your strategies and tactics:

1. What will be your general strategy or approach for this negotiation effort?

   _____

   _____

2. What additional strategies are you prepared to use, should they become necessary as you reassess your position during the session?

   _____

   _____

3. What tactics are you prepared to use?

   _____

   _____

   _____

   _____

   _____

Identify strategies/tactics likely to be used by the other side:

List the strategies and tactics you anticipate. Then note how you plan to react or respond to each.

   _____

   _____

   _____

   _____

   _____

   _____

   _____

   _____

Chapter 6 Checkpoints

Match the strategy or tactic in column A to the appropriate description in column B. (Hint: Some items in column A may be used more than once.)

Column A

A. Stonewalling.

B. Impulsive change.

C. Gotcha.

D. Dodge.

E. High ball/ low ball.

F. Emotional outburst.

G. Scrooge.

H. Mother-May-I.

Column B

____ 1. The other side says they have to check with headquarters before they can agree to a schedule change.

____ 2. You begin the negotiation by making a rather outrageous demand for a 25 percent pay raise.

____ 3. You cancel a current contract, then resume negotiations with the same company for future work.

____ 4. The other side's negotiator shakes his finger under your nose and suggests that you'd better watch your step.

____ 5. No matter what tactics you try, your worthy opponents do not respond; they give you the silent treatment.

____ 6. Despite your best efforts, the other side keeps postponing a decision on the conditions for negotiation. You can't even get them to the table.

____ 7. You have been the nice guy throughout the negotiations; now you've decided to get tough.

____ 8. The other side has been saying they are not really interested in the additional acreage you're offering for sale; now suddenly they've brought it into the negotiation process.

____ 9. The other side has been giving in very quickly to a series of small concessions; now they've dug in their heels.

____ **10.** You've offered a rock-bottom price for a houseful of antiques.

____ **11.** You've been instructed not to "give away the farm," so you've been very stingy with concessions.

____ **12.** You've got to beg the plant to reserve the units you're about to sell because the customer wants immediate delivery.

____ **13.** Your opponent seems determined to make you give in before he will. It's almost a test of strength.

____ **14.** You've decided to make the other side sweat a little, so you postpone your next round of negotiations.

____ **15.** You absolutely cannot accept one of the terms the other side insists on, so you avoid discussing that issue and focus on other areas for dialogue.

____ **16.** When you suggest adjourning the negotiations because you are stymied, the other side stomps off in a huff.

Checkpoint 6 Feedback

Check your answers with those given below.

1. H
2. E
3. C
4. F
5. F
6. A
7. B
8. D
9. B
10. E
11. G
12. H
13. G
14. A
15. D
16. F

7 | Negotiating Like a Pro

This chapter will help you to:

- Apply techniques to develop agreement.
- Develop a positive attitude toward negotiation.

Linda:

Tom, I want to go the the reunion. My plans are made. It would be awful to have to cancel now.

Tom:

I know that, Linda. You've been talking about it for weeks. But I've also made plans. I've paid for a cruise, and canceling would cost a bundle.

Linda:

We've got to come up with something. How can we both get what we want?

Tom:

Let's stop defending our positions. Why don't we put our heads together and brainstorm for ideas while we eat. Then, while we have dessert, we'll consider every option—even the ones that sound silly at first.

Linda:

OK, Tom. At this point I'll try anything that might get us out of this situation. How do we get started? ∎

MOVING TOWARD A RESOLUTION

In the last chapter you began exploring strategies and tactics used in Phase Two of the negotiation process. This chapter offers some additional techniques and tips for moving toward a resolution in a negotiating session.

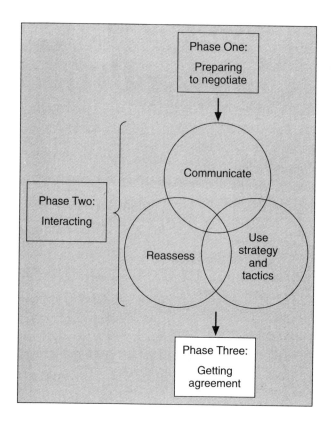

GETTING AGREEMENT

The ultimate goal of any negotiation is to reach an agreement that satisfies the needs of all parties. Sometimes that can be achieved easily. However, in some cases, it's hard to resolve differences and forge a working relationship. Experienced negotiators agree that there are some things you can do to improve your chances of success. Here are some tips to help you get agreement.

Seek Alternatives

As a negotiator, you are always in search of alternatives—a variety of ways for meeting the needs of both sides. But even good negotiators can run out of ideas. Negotiations will quickly stall without new alternatives to consider.

Put yourself in this situation. Your negotiation session is a stalemate. Neither party is willing to make concessions. Nothing productive seems to be happening. Your ideas have all been tried and found wanting. Take a brainstorming break.

Invite all parties to participate in a brainstorming session. Brainstorming generates new ideas or creative approaches to a problem. In a brainstorming session, everyone is encouraged to come up with suggestions, ideas, possible solutions—no matter how wild or crazy they may initially seem. These ideas are recorded on a flipchart, but are not discussed during the brainstorming session. The emphasis here is on getting ideas to surface, not on evaluating them. Once you've got a new supply of ideas, then you can go back and begin examining these new alternatives to see if they might lead to a mutually satisfactory negotiated solution.

Find Common Ground

For some reason, negotiations tend to focus on the differences between parties. There is another way of looking at the situation. Remember the difference between the optimist and the pessimist? One saw the glass as half full, and the other saw it as half empty. That idea can be extended to negotiators. Some negotiators see only the distance between two parties in a negotiation, and others see the common ground.

Find the common ground, and you'll find an excellent starting point for negotiations to move forward. It's easy to lose your perspective in a negotiation. Before you know it you're focusing on positions—defending your position and assaulting the other side's posltion. You need to step back and take a look at the common ground. Look for ways of bringing the sides closer together. You may have values in common. You may share a common goal. You may even be worried about the same issues. If you can find the common ground, you can use it as a foundation for building a working relationship.

Use an Agent

Sometimes it's a wise decision to let an agent do the negotiating for you. If you know the negotiations will involve intensely emotional issues, you may be better off having someone take over the job for you. An example is the role of the attorney in a divorce proceeding. Often both parties are too involved at the emotional level to negotiate a property settlement with a cool head and fair hand. Their attorneys act as negotiating agents.

Another example is the use of a designated representative as negotiator. Every worker cannot possibly negotiate his or her own wages and benefits. Instead, for example, labor unions or trade associations might have designated staff represent the general membership in negotiations. They are acting as agents for their constituency.

In addition, some situations challenge your feelings of competence even if you are not emotionally involved in the matter at hand. Most of us, for example, would not feel comfortable negotiating international trade rights or trying to get agreement about the exploration of space. These matters are beyond average technical knowledge and require special expertise. These complex issues may involve negotiating teams consisting entirely of agents.

If you anticipate problems in handling the negotiations, consider using an agent. The agent can shield you from personal assaults and emotional attacks. The agent can also provide expertise or experience that you do not have.

Buy Time to Think

It's hard to think on your feet. When you are sitting across the table from the other party, you may find it difficult to respond quickly to every tactic and trick the opposing side throws at you in a session. If you can't think of a way to respond, the normal reaction is panic. You stammer and stutter, sweat and worry. You just don't know what to do, or you cannot decide on your next step. Buy time to think.

You need a safety valve that will let some of the steam escape from the pressure cooker. You need a moment—or an hour, a day, a week—to get your thoughts together. Try any of these tactics to buy time.

- Get up and move around the room a bit.
- Suggest a coffee break.
- Say you'll address the issue as soon as you get back from the restroom.
- Indicate that you've got a pressing appointment, but you'd like to reconvene after lunch.
- Call for an official time out.
- Leave the room and the building. Take a walk outside.
- Telephone a colleague for advice and counsel.
- Make any excuse you want, but buy time to think.

Defer to Standards

Negotiating parties may get stuck over whose version of the facts is true or whose proposal is most reasonable or acceptable. If you can come up with a set of objective criteria or impartial standards for measuring acceptability, you can usually move the negotiation forward over the obstacle.

As you negotiate a settlement for storm damage to your home, for example, your insurance adjuster may refer to a formula in the company's procedures manual, and that results in a figure too low to be acceptable to you. You, on the other hand, may refer to the actual cost to rebuild or repair in your community, evidenced by several bids from licensed local contractors. That approach, however, won't be acceptable to the adjustor. What's wrong with this picture?

Each side has appealed to a different set of standards. Each believes its standards should be acceptable to the other side. Clearly, the parties must find a different set of standards or another set of objective criteria to come to an agreement. If possible, establish agreement about acceptable standards early in the negotiation. Be cautious about accepting standards or criteria that are unfamiliar to you or that are likely to be biased in the other side's favor. In order to work, standards *must* be impartial.

Make It Easy to Agree

In a disagreement, you can sometimes force the other side to give in by applying more pressure, by being an adept negotiator, or by eliminating all their options. Unfortunately, the resulting agreement is likely to carry negative feelings with it. Consider another approach. Make it easy for the other side to go along with your suggestions or ideas. Give the other party a way of saving face. Here are some examples.

Imagine that you are asking for an exception to the family leave policy at your company. The personnel manager quickly responds that there will be no exceptions to policy; after all, that's what a policy means—the same standards for everyone. How can you get past this obstacle in your path to a negotiated agreement? You might try pointing out that conditions have changed since the policy was drawn up in the 1970s. This offers the personnel manager a logical basis for reconsidering the fallibility of the company's standards. It opens the door for you to make your case, and it allows the manager a graceful way of backing off from an earlier position.

Suppose you are leasing communications equipment for your firm. Your manager has told you a maximum cost figure. You've found the perfect combination of equipment for your company's needs, and you've got a deal made with the salesperson. But it costs more than the manager allocated, and you're nervous about explaining the overage to your manager. The salesperson can make it easy for you to buy. He arranges the financial details so the lease payment total is within the figure you received from your manager, providing the firm will make an additional cash downpayment. It's a compromise, of course. However, when the salesperson volunteers to go with you to your manager and explain the added value received for the investment, he also makes it easy for you to save face with your manager.

As you suggest options in negotiations, consider how they look from the other side. Look for ways of making it easy for the other party to agree. Offer escape routes that tactfully let the other side step back from an untenable position. Plant the seed of an idea, and let the other side nurture it until they take ownership of it.

Develop a Partnership

As you negotiate, think in terms of building a partnership. This concept of working together as partners illustrates many of the ideas we've covered in this book. As a partner, you are in a better position to:

- Seek alternatives and brainstorm for options.
- Overcome obstacles to meet everyone's needs.
- Arrive at mutually acceptable solutions for win–win results.

Never lose sight of your primary objective in negotiations—getting agreement. If you work together to achieve that objective, your chances of success increase dramatically.

Think about It

Here are some important principles of negotiation. Where do you stand on each of them? Circle A for agree or D for Disagree.

    A   **D**   **1.** All parties in a negotiation want to win.

    A   **D**   **2.** A successful negotiation means both parties are satisfied.

    A   **D**   **3.** Negotiation is not a contest; it's an alliance for making progress toward needs and goals.

    A   **D**   **4.** When parties in a negotiation work as partners, they tend to try harder to make the negotiation succeed.

    A   **D**   **5.** A win-win negotiation is preferred over a win-lose situation.

A   D   6. If all parties are satisfied with the results of the negotiation, they are more willing to work together in the future.

A   D   7. Cooperation is usually a better strategy than confrontation.

A   D   8. Negotiation necessarily involves both giving and getting on both sides.

A   D   9. Flexibility is usually a better approach than standing firm against all odds.

A   D   10. Compromising in negotiation is not a sign of weakness.

A   D   11. Negotiating skills become better with practice.

A   D   12. To be a successful negotiator, you need to know your opponent, and you must also know yourself.

How did you do? More A's than D's shows you recognize essential elements of good negotiation.

7

Chapter 7 Checkpoints

Fill in the appropriate word or phrase.

1. When you need to come up with some fresh ideas or options in a negotiating session, you might use a technique called _____ _____.

2. Even when parties seem to be radically opposed to one another, the wise negotiator will seek out _____ ground.

3. An _____ is another person who negotiates for you or represents your interests in a negotiation.

4. When you're emotionally involved or intellectually uncomfortable to do your own negotiating, you might consider using an _____.

5. During a negotiating session, you may find it difficult to think or react quickly under pressure. Make an excuse that will give you _____ and enable you to gather your thoughts.

6. Negotiations may stall if you run out of ideas or _____.

7. In negotiating, you might focus on your differences, or you could choose to focus on _____.

8. If you put yourself into the other side's shoes, then you'll understand why lt's important to make it _____ for the other side to agree with your proposal.

9. The prudent negotiator offers the other side an escape route that lets them _____.

10. Standards used in a negotiation should be _____.

11. Successful negotiators attempt to build a _____ with the other parties to work together for a satisfactory resolution to their problems or issues.

Checkpoint 7 Feedback

Check your answers.

1. Brainstorming.
2. Common.
3. Agent.
4. Agent.
5. Time to think.
6. Alternatives (or options).
7. Your common ground or similarities.
8. Easy.
9. Save face or back away gracefully.
10. Mutually agreeable or objective.
11. Partnership.

Post-Test

Mark each item T or F.

_____   1. A negotiation is a contest between opposing sides.

_____   2. Negotiation always results in a winning side and a losing side.

_____   3. Negotiation is a means of forging an agreement between parties.

_____   4. Negotiation is a communication process between two or more people in which they consider alternatives to arrive at mutually agreeable solutions or reach mutually satisfactory objectives.

_____   5. Everyone negotiates.

_____   6. When a perceived conflict exists between parties, the situation is ripe for negotiation.

_____   7. Negotiation is a civilized method of conflict resolution.

_____   8. The true goal of negotiating is getting as much as you can for your own side.

_____   9. Cooperation is preferable to confrontation as an approach to negotiating.

_____   10. Negotiation is you and the other side working together.

_____   11. With negotiation, conflicts may be resolved through compromise.

_____   12. The three critical elements in negotiation are knowledge, power, and compromise.

_____   13. In negotiation, the more you know about the other side, the better off you will be.

_____   14. In negotiation, what you don't know can—and probably will—hurt you.

_____   15. When facing a deadline, most people make their decisions quickly in order to have plenty of time left to meet the deadline.

_____   16. Strength in a negotiation may come as a result of knowledge.

_____ 17. The balance of power in a negotiating session is dynamic.

_____ 18. If one side has all the perceived power in a negotiation, the negotiation session will come to a natural close.

_____ 19. If both sides perceive that power is about equal, the negotiation will move toward a negotiated close.

_____ 20. If power is radically out of balance in a negotiation, the resulting settlement will probably not be mutually satisfactory.

_____ 21. The party with the earliest deadline in a negotiation has the stronger position.

_____ 22. The party with the most accurate and relevant knowledge is likely to prevail in a negotiation.

_____ 23. In order to achieve a compromise, parties in a negotiation must attempt to balance or share power.

_____ 24. Power may be real or assumed.

_____ 25. Power is effective only if it is acknowledged.

_____ 26. Power must be used in order to be effective in a negotiation.

_____ 27. Using power in a negotiation carries some risks of alienating the other side.

_____ 28. Time constraints or deadlines tend to increase pressure on negotiators.

_____ 29. The first phase of the negotiation process is preparation.

_____ 30. The second phase of the process is the actual negotiating session.

_____ 31. The third phase of the negotiation process is getting agreement.

_____ 32. Communications skills are important in the second phase of the negotiating process.

_____ 33. During Phase Two, you'll be applying various strategies and tactics to advance the negotiation toward a close.

_____ 34. In negotiation, you should talk more than half the time.

_____ **35.** Preparing for negotiation is limited to identifying your own bottom line.

_____ **36.** A good negotiator is a person who understands people, is confident, and remains open-minded.

_____ **37.** Your bottom line in a negotiation is the point at which you believe there is no point in continuing the effort.

_____ **38.** Knowing the other side's bottom line can help you think of options or alternatives.

_____ **39.** Direct and indirect questions may be used to gather information during a negotiating session.

_____ **40.** Observing the other side's gestures and facial expressions may give you clues to their feelings and emotions.

_____ **41.** Intentionally delaying the progress of negotiations is called stonewalling.

_____ **42.** Radical changes in behavior or approach may be an attempt to use the impulsive change strategy.

_____ **43.** The dodge is a variation on the impulsive change.

_____ **44.** An emotional outburst typically unsettles your opponent in a negotiation.

_____ **45.** High-ball/low-ball tactics are no longer acceptable practices for negotiations.

POST-TEST FEEDBACK

1. F	2. F	3. T	4. T	5. T	6. T	7. T	8. F
9. T	10. T	11. T	12. F	13. T	14. T	15. F	16. T
17. T	18. T	19. T	20. T	21. F	22. T	23. T	24. T
25. T	26. F	27. T	28. T	29. T	30. T	31. T	32. T
33. T	34. F	35. F	36. T	37. T	38. T	39. T	40. T
41. T	42. T	43. F	44. T	45. F			

Negotiating Skills Inventory

Find out how good a negotiator you are! First, analyze your negotiating skills with this personal inventory. If you find that you can't score a 4 or 5 on each item, take time to review these skills. Then develop a P-l-P (personalized improvement plan) using the Skill Maintenance Checklist at the end of this book.

For each skill listed, circle a number to estimate your own skill level.

5 = Excellent   4 = Very Good   3 = Good   2 = Fair   1 = Poor

From Chapters 1 and 2

1 2 3 4 5   **1.** Avoiding confrontation over issues.

1 2 3 4 5   **2.** Encouraging cooperation to resolve issues.

1 2 3 4 5   **3.** Focusing on similarities and common grounds.

1 2 3 4 5   **4.** Minimizing differences or working around obstacles.

1 2 3 4 5   **5.** Recognizing opportunities to negotiate.

1 2 3 4 5   **6.** Thinking of negotiations in a positive way.

1 2 3 4 5   **7.** Believing you can succeed in negotiations.

1 2 3 4 5   **8.** Developing agreement.

1 2 3 4 5   **9.** Looking for ways both parties can be winners.

1 2 3 4 5   **10.** Working together with the other side.

1 2 3 4 5   **11.** Using knowledge or information effectively.

1 2 3 4 5   **12.** Managing time or deadline pressures.

1 2 3 4 5   **13.** Striving for a balance of power.

1 2 3 4 5   **14.** Sticking to your own bottom line.

1 2 3 4 5   **15.** Wielding power effectively.

From Chapter 3

1 2 3 4 5   **16.** Preparing for negotiation sessions.

1 2 3 4 5   **17.** Listening actively during negotiations.

1 2 3 4 5   **18.** Using tactful questions.

1 2 3 4 5   **19.** Carefully observing the other side.

1 2 3 4 5   **20.** Reassessing your position during negotiations.

1 2 3 4 5   **21.** Understanding people in negotiations.

1 2 3 4 5   **22.** Being confident.

1 2 3 4 5   **23.** Remaining open-minded during negotiations.

1 2 3 4 5   **24.** Remaining calm during sessions.

1 2 3 4 5   **25.** Seeking options (alternatives).

From Chapter 4

1 2 3 4 5   **26.** Identifying motives, objectives, or needs.

1 2 3 4 5   **27.** Assessing starting positions.

1 2 3 4 5   **28.** Establishing your own bottom line.

1 2 3 4 5   **29.** Gathering information about the other side.

1 2 3 4 5   **30.** Estimating the other side's bottom line.

From Chapter 5

1 2 3 4 5   **31.** Formulating direct questions.

1 2 3 4 5   **32.** Using indirect questions effectively.

1 2 3 4 5   **33.** Framing questions to achieve a desired effect.

1 2 3 4 5   **34.** Listening attentively.

1 2 3 4 5   **35.** Interpreting gestures.

From Chapter 6

1 2 3 4 5   **36.** Responding to stonewalling.

1 2 3 4 5   **37.** Responding to the impulsive change.

1 2 3 4 5   **38.** Responding to the gotcha approach.

1 2 3 4 5   **39.** Managing the dodge.

1 2 3 4 5   **40.** Recognizing high-ball/low-ball tactics.

1 2 3 4 5   **41.** Handling emotional outbursts.

1 2 3 4 5   **42.** Responding to the Ebenezer Scrooge tactic.

1 2 3 4 5   **43.** Responding to the mother-may-I approach.

1 2 3 4 5   **44.** Selecting appropriate strategies and tactics.

1 2 3 4 5   **45.** Reacting effectively to strategies and tactics.

From Chapter 7

1 2 3 4 5   **46.** Moving the negotiations toward a close.

1 2 3 4 5   **47.** Getting agreement.

1 2 3 4 5   **48.** Finding common ground.

1 2 3 4 5   **49.** Using an agent.

1 2 3 4 5   **50.** Buying time to think during negotiations.

1 2 3 4 5   **51.** Deferring to standards.

1 2 3 4 5   **52.** Making it easy for the other side to agree.

1 2 3 4 5   **53.** Developing a partnership.

Business Skills Express Series

This growing series of books addresses a broad range of key business skills and topics to meet the needs of employees, human resource departments, and training consultants.

To obtain information about these and other Business Skills Express books, please call IRWIN Professional Publishing toll free at: 1-800-634-3966.

Effective Performance Management
ISBN   1-55623-867-3

Hiring the Best
ISBN   1-55623-865-7

Writing that Works
ISBN   1-55623-856-8

Customer Service Excellence
ISBN   1-55623-969-6

Writing for Business Results
ISBN   1-55623-854-1

Powerful Presentation Skills
ISBN   1-55623-870-3

Meetings that Work
ISBN   1-55623-866-5

Effective Teamwork
ISBN   1-55623-880-0

Time Management
ISBN   1-55623-888-6

Assertiveness Skills
ISBN   1-55623-857-6

Motivation at Work
ISBN   1-55623-868-1

Overcoming Anxiety at Work
ISBN   1-55623-869-X

Positive Politics at Work
ISBN   1-55623-879-7

Telephone Skills at Work
ISBN   1-55623-858-4

Managing Conflict at Work
ISBN   1-55623-890-8

The New Supervisor: Skills for Success
ISBN   1-55623-762-6

The *Americans with Disabilities Act*: What Supervisors Need to Know
ISBN   1-55623-889-4

Managing the Demands of Work and Home
ISBN   0-7863-0221-6

Effective Listening Skills
ISBN   0-7863-0102-4

Goal Management at Work
ISBN   0-7863-0225-9

Positive Attitudes at Work
ISBN   0-7863-0100-8

Supervising the Difficult Employee
ISBN   0-7863-0219-4

Cultural Diversity in the Workplace
ISBN   0-7863-0125-2

Managing Organizational Change
ISBN   0-7863-0162-7

Negotiating for Business Results
ISBN   0-7863-0114-7

Practical Business Communication
ISBN   0-7863-0227-5

High Performance Speaking
ISBN   0-7863-0222-4

Delegation Skills
ISBN   0-7863-0105-9

Coaching Skills: A Guide for Supervisors
ISBN   0-7863-0220-8

Customer Service and the Telephone
ISBN   0-7863-0224-0

Total Quality Selling
ISBN   0-7863-0274-7

Creativity at Work
ISBN   0-7863-0223-2

Effective Interpersonal Relationships
ISBN   0-7863-0255-0

The Participative Leader
ISBN   0-7863-0252-6

Building Customer Loyalty
ISBN   0-7863-0253-4

Getting and Staying Organized
ISBN   0-7863-0254-2

Business Etiquette
ISBN   0-7863-0273-9